Ink
&
a Whiskey Back

A Collection of Poems

A. Goodberry

NFB Publishing
Buffalo, New York

ISBN: 978-1-7338764-1-4

Ink & a Whiskey Back/Goodberry-1st ed.

1. Poems. 2. Poetry. 3. Verse. 4. Female Voice
4. Goodberry

NFB Publishing/Amelia Press
<<<>>>
119 Dorchester Road
Buffalo, New York 14213
          For more information please visit
          nfbpublishing.com

To me.

I want to read this if I live to be old, remembering how overly dramatic, thrilling, and scandalous a life I had.

&

To you

I hope you'll come across this someday, and wonder which lines are yours.

Sweat clung to her collarbone
Like dew on blades of grass
At morning's first light

She could smell him in her hair
On her skin and throughout the sheets
Engulfing them both like waves
On a sea; they could drift away

Sandalwood, bergamot and cedar
Carried her afar as she breathed him in
But they were closer than their fingers interlocked

So long as they stayed this way
Not wanting or needing
No misleading
Love would last eternally

Sea of sheets part
Limbs belonging again to their own body
The space between them now a chasm

She slides her jeans up over her legs
Not washed a few wears over
Had given the denim a familiar worn feeling
Hugging each of her curves

She walked home
She didn't brush her hair
Or wash last night's makeup from her face

She slept

All the time you spent wondering

You could have been wandering

Exploring, discovering

Free

Sparks singe the hair on my forearm

Kisses from the fire

I lay near

Cool ashes rise like ghosts

Carried away by the night's breeze

Along with my thoughts

Embers glow, as do the eyes of a fox

Rustling through fern

He watches me

Plumes of smoke dance across my face

Stinging my eyes; they water

I don't turn away

The wood crackles as the flames consume it

Insects begin their symphony

I listen

I'll never again be as free as tonight

Alone in this wood

The fire and me

I'll remember how you smell

Maybe not exactly, but the way it made me feel

I have memories of us that never came to be

They were there though,

When I breathed in the scent of you

Where your neck and shoulder meet

I lived countless days within each touch of your lips to mine

Those memories all wishes

Those days all dreams

Evaporated like the notes of your cologne

Wingtips and whiskey

I feel the weight of you on top of me

You loved the way I wanted you

Now I can't stop, though I try to

Buffalo check and black jeans

I hear your voice in my dreams

You wanted me to hold you

I still would, oh how I long to

Keep with you my villainous laughter

I'll take with me your grizzly sounds

I hope you'll miss my hands on your back

Fingers through your hair and beard

You should know I long for your head nuzzled into my chest

Your body getting heavy as you fall asleep

Be disappointed in yourself for losing someone

Who gave you tissues for your glove box

I'll be somber over someone

I knew I could not keep

With every word I write

A piece of you leaves me

Pouring the memory of you

From my insides onto paper

Purging you until my pen runs dry

Feeling my soul restored

Forgetting now, no memory

Of how you could've hurt me

I must've done it to myself

Like the wind traveling

With no certain destination

But rushing there just the same

As free and wild as it moves

Ever changing its course

I don't know where I'm going

I'm sure I'll find my way

She liked the idea of a lover

More than having one

She wanted only to press her lips against his

To feel his hand on the small of her back

The other cradling her head

All the while their bodies more tangled than before

But she did not want to belong to anyone

Or worry about their opinion of her

The way she styled her hair

The clothes that clung to her body

Showing more than he would like others to see

She would revel in the moments

That they consumed each other with suffocating passion

As their hearts raced in climax

The world falling away and her legs getting weak

He'd run his fingertips over her skin

As she slips into dream

She is alone though

There isn't a lover she could find

That would love her

For all she is

Wild, unapologetic, quixotic

Not a part of 'we'

I feel nothing and I feel fine

The planets don't worry about their paths in orbit

I don't concern myself with when I'll see you again

You came into my life and back out

Like the waxing and waning of the moon

My life has not changed

I am the sun

Constant, burning and bright

You only had light because I shone on you

My world revolves around me

You only follow it

I remain the center

I feel nothing and I feel fine

Kiss me with a passion

My lips have never known

Let me feel the way you've longed for me

Since we've been apart

Give me your hands on my body

Hold me like you own me

Make me yours for just a little while

Leave me again tomorrow

Droplets splash onto the window sill

Warm summer showers in June

Washes my thoughts away

With the grime and gravel from the street

He lays still next to me

Unaware of the rain coming down

I look at him

Differently than when we're in conversation

Taking in all the things about him

That I've become complacent to

Full lips, that when making love

Press against my neck and collarbone

I can feel their warmth even now

His squared chin and hard jawline

Mirror the strength within him

The rain comes down harder now

I close the window

As the storm grows outside

I admire the definition of his chest and shoulders

Most likely tired from the weeks work

He carries me around our small apartment anyway

Thunder breaks the quiet of our room

He stirs, looking up at me

A gaze so intense, fixed upon me now

Lightning flashes across the sky

And in his eyes

He draws my body closer to his

We become the tempest

Take me to the end of your love

Where you are your weakest

I want to see inside of you

Find where you pull your strength from

Bring me to the beginning of hope

Show me what you wish for

I want to know your conscience

So I may realize your intentions

Your necklace gets in the way

Pressing against my cheek

Colder than I am inside

You don't feel like him or have his scent

But little by little you replace him

Without even knowing

You're not the lover he was

But this is what I need right now

I close my eyes and let him go

I use your body for what I want

For I'm no longer wanted

I don't remember you getting undressed

Just the weight of you on my breast

My cheek on your chest

How you'd breathe after sex

We waited so long for this

After five years, a reunion

Messages exchanged

Drunken late night phone calls

But when you reach the peak

All you have left is the decent

And the memory of what you've done

I never wanted to keep you

I only wished to breathe you in

Let my lashes brush across your skin

For a few nights each season

Until my heart stopped beating

The smell of the fire as it clashed with your cologne was intoxicating

Your heavy hand, as you rested it

Spanned wider than my leg

Fingers settling between my thighs

My cheeks were flush from the hot embers glowing in front of us

You set the rest of me ablaze

Perhaps a wild thing runs full stride

Looking to be caught

Comes out only under the cover of night

To liven the chase for the hunter

Clinging to shadows, treading lightly

In anticipation

Of course you should not believe this to be true

The thing is wild

Just like me

You will not happen upon me

In your snare

Dripping from your lips and fingertips

My love

Deep inside and it fills me up

Your love

I've exhausted my lust for power tonight

Take me, pick me up, toss me down

Do what you'd like

Control me

If all you would give me is a kiss

I would take it

For hours on end

I would relish in the luxury of those lips

You'd share with me

Mine pushing into yours

Never ceasing to be ever closer

Desperately looking to find truth

On one another's tongue

Give me your lips on all the places

You love me most

Then give me all of you as a man

When I can no longer stand it

I would've liked to say goodbye

To the crease above your brow

Tension in your back

The heft of your arm across me as you slept

Goodbye to holding me so close

I couldn't breathe

As we finished

What a sordid love we have

Like pages of a book

Enjoyed by others when we're apart

Not whole unless we're together

A warm breeze runs through the grass

Rushing up and over the hill I lay on

Carrying with it, notes of lilac and magnolia

My skin awash with sun

I close my eyes

Feel it dance across my face

As it finds it's way through the leaves of a black walnut tree

I spend so much time alive at night

Neon signs illuminating me in all my revelry

I've all but forgotten

How the light of day makes me feel

Washed clean of the moonlit madness

Of my whiskey soaked meetings with you

The dissolution of the 'us' we never were

Was so anticlimactic

I don't know whether I miss you

Or long for a grande finalé

Maybe that's why I've done this

Unforgivable thing

To give myself the ending you wouldn't

Access but no ownership

A nervous smile

A wink

Flirtation in type and nude photos sent

But no follow through

You like being wanted

I enjoy a chase

I love the way

You put your hand around my neck

Taking the life right out of me

But kissing me all the while

Like you've loved me your whole life

And are just now knowing

The pleasure of my lips

My hair

Piercings

Tattoos

Perhaps my attitude

Or what you perceive my lifestyle to be

Whatever it is

That somewhere in your mind

Puts you above me

Just know

Everyone slums it

Once in awhile

I was looking for something with you

That I'd lost on him

A sense of excitement

From being with someone new

A little trouble

Because our tryst was taboo

Only I can't grasp it

I'll not walk you to the door

You know the way out

We've done this before

Take your half drunk bottle of whiskey

When you go

But leave behind

Traces of your sex and cologne

In my sheets

Your skin smells like tequila from last night

My hair like sandalwood and cigarettes

I've come in sweats and sneakers

You're dressed the same

Pulling at these clothes

Our mouths finding each other's

Like we've done this before

Tangled in limbs and a feather down cover

You share with another

My heart races as you kiss me far below it

Everything about this is wrong

Secret from even closest friends

A betrayal of the ones we should be with

Somehow it feels better because of

Not in spite of it

The way you move

Is a shadow of my former lover

Your friend

It's almost comforting

Your bodies mirror each other in bed

But your lips

They leave a signature of their own

Across mine

And more often

I'm careful not to leave marks on you

You don't being to me

After the tension between us subsides

We lay together

We laugh

Jovial bliss

•••

We catch our breath

Take time to admire

The ginger in your beard

The freckle on my bottom lip

I trace your tattoos

You think you're still drunk

I have somewhere to be

Still we have our fill once more

In your car, you kiss me one last time

For now

A knowing grin works it's way across your face

A flash of excitement in your eyes

This shouldn't have happened at all

But we know it will again

The words won't come

The way I did with you

Because you want this secret

But everything must have an end

And only I know when I'll tell

Burning bridges and dousing them with whiskey

I'll set this town ablaze before leaving you behind

The memory of my kisses like hot ash in your mouth

Longing to lay with me again makes your king size a bed of hot coals

But company of another does nothing to ignite you

For you have already been consumed by the inferno that I am

Rebuild what I've scorched while I'm gone

I'll be back to light up your cold December

I'll not belong to anyone

I love the thrill of something new

Remember when we were young

I met you by the creek

How shy I was then

Unsure of myself; my body

I want again that moment

You descending the stairs to a basement party

Older now but I was still foolish enough

To believe we'd be real

After the car show; smoke from burnouts gone

I sat in your lap to steal your attention

What a web to be ensnared in

Working together on the beach

A sweeter escape, I have not found

But our hearts knew easy love stalls even you

Maybe I'm learning these lessons to appreciate finding you

I think I'm finding I'll always be happy alone

I always thought you'd be around

For me to lean on

I suppose we all have that person

And lose them

That loss forcing us up on our own two

Steadying now on these spindly legs

All this time keeps slipping away from me

I see you everywhere

If you're going to be gone

I wish you'd go away completely

I've been made to be strong all my life

So much, that the only thing I fear

Is how weak I am for you

Still I cannot bring myself

To let you know I love you

To tell you how I want the time

You used to give to me so freely

I'm letting you fade away from my day to day

When I want you to stay

And so it goes

I will not say, you will not know

We will not be

You and me

I speak out to you, the stars I gaze upon

My melancholy soliloquy

If I'm to always be alone, what I wouldn't give

For all the days to be nights

Sinking ever deeper into the slough of despond

I do not feel the weight as heavily

When I look up to all of you

The sense of whimsy I get when you twinkle

Puts the light back in my eyes

Until I remember that you're all dead

Like me inside

An audience of celestial ghosts

Listening to my woes

Your fingers run across my skin

Like a match on phosphorous

You spark a need within me

Give me your gasoline

A dozen kisses from your lips

Licking up my legs like flames

You light me up

I'm dripping kerosene

You pull up your black boxer briefs

I only now notice that you didn't take off your socks

I giggle to myself; just loud enough that you heard me

Your eyes flit over to me, narrowing on their target

You slap my butt and scoop me up

You settle us down on the bed

Making that grunting sound now

While I rub my hands over your neck and shoulders

You pull me closer and press your lips to mine

I feel so small; your hand spans the width of my back

You tell me you feel safe with me

I wonder then, why you didn't stay

You've already gotten what you wanted

Still you send me good morning's

Tell me I'm beautiful

It could all be a ploy

I'd be lying if I said you didn't make me smile

Make my days a little brighter

My nights more inspired

I'll never regret you

Never forget you

A little time with you went a long way

Three times a charmer

I'll never rid myself of the way you felt

It was all the things you said

Built this attachment I can't shake

I'm not sure why you put in so much effort

When you already knew I wanted you

I suppose a game of cat and mouse

Is no fun without a chase

But you've already made your kill

And I'm still running

What a pity

I realized too late

I was the prey all along

Sure I fell for you

I fall for everyone

I want to

What is the fun

In making love

Without passion

Of course I'll be left wounded

I left myself open to it

But it's my heart to break

What is love without loss

What is life without love

Your lips against mine

Bring me to another place

You bite mine

I let go

Don't loose another arrow

You've already shot me down

Watch my eyes dull

Once sparkling as diamonds

Now flat as glass

Make me your trophy

Hang me in a room seldom used

Forget about how beautiful and free

I once was

Before you made your kill

How deep is this abyss

And why do you call it love

You started a song in my heart

Though now it is broken

The band plays on

If you were a part of that night sky

That I do so love to fix my gaze upon

You would not be the moon

Changing each day

On some occasions hidden away from view

You would not be a star

One of an uncountable collection of lights

Barely distinguishable from another

You, my darling, would be the black of the sky

Filling all the space in between

You are everywhere and fill all the space in me

If it should be

That you are a dream

And the sun should break my slumber

I hope to see you again

In the morning

Next to me

I think of deleting all of you

And I shudder

Something like a chill

To my already winter imprisoned self

Maybe I'm even colder, now you've gone

You knew my heart was weak

I was not well

But you starved me, Skinny Lover, anyway

My scenery was lush and in bloom with you

A beckoning oasis within my desert of faltering self worth

But even so it was all a mirage, because as it turned out

You never saw it

What a dirty little trick is doubt

Snuffing out the countless skips of your heartbeat

For the worry of a tragedy that may never come to harm you

I'd like to stitch up the corners of your mouth

And eyes

With kisses soft and sweet

So that you would always be smiling

Sewn by my lips into happiness

I feel that your absence has taken the air from my lungs

But I'm lost in the delirium of sleep deprivation

What chance, to be lovesick and ill

I wonder if I'll break from this feeling as from a fever

Agonizing, then suddenly gone

With only but a cool shiver of a memory

My kisses must have been dreadful

Arsenic on my lips

Tongue dripping with motor oil

Gentle bites on your neck filling you with venom

It must have made you sick being near me

Radiation seeping from my personality

Nuclear fallout leaving you despondent

Too many words always spilling from my mouth

Like formaldehyde pouring into your ears

Encasing your brain from having to listen

Holding me had to be painful

Wrapping your arms around shards of glass

Running your hands across my skin

Bleeding you out

In my skull

My brain

Always creeping, crawling

Each leg tap tap tapping in time

The rhythmic pattern of my madness

A centipede creates a deafening chatter

The segments of its body each a mistake that I've made

And its ever growing, stretching

On and on and on

More legs

Pulling its slithering, writhing body

Through my mind

Mouthparts mangling, chewing through reason

My mind is forever suffering the incessant humming of flies

They prod and poke and lick

The folds and bends of my brain

Triggering a memory

Making me twitch, tick, stutter

Fucking flies

Wasps will sting

And snakes will strike

That all seems so obvious

Yet here you are

Putting your heart

In my hands

If you bruise my heart

I'll devour yours; still beating

You've changed me

For the better?

Maybe

But only because steel

Is forged in fire

And you burn me

Still

What a pity

You no longer like my poems

And I chose the kindest words

To write for you

I could've cut you to ribbons

Shearing away at you in prose

Smile gleaming

Eyes gleaning what's left of you

Strands of red they fall down around me

I gather them up in my hands

And watch them come down again

And the bare bones of you

Hollowed and aching

Make such a beautifully haunting sound

As the wind from my breath

Blows through them

When your knees would finally come to bend

Bringing you down onto snow laden ground

With me

I would stand

I would stare into those lackluster eyes

Choosing this time

To write my last line across your throat

With a goodbye

As sharp as a first string

Around your neck

Friend or enemy

You should think

Of which you'd rather be

To me

My heart's on crooked

And it's beating slow

I can wait for days

But if left to me

I choose foe

If revenge is a dish

Best served cold

Let it snow

Let it snow

Let it snow

All the music sad

I don't even mind

That nights have turned cold

But when the lovers crooning

Swoon for you

Even still when their notes go flat

And back to black

I feel you in every lyric told

I know I'll never find

The together we once had

I will never lose you

You're here

You are my pain

You linger

Your ghost drifts

Out from the speakers

Haunting me with memories

Still not giving me a reason

Why I wasn't worth

You

I'm sorry that I didn't know

I didn't know what we were doing

What you needed

It was so simple

I didn't even see it

I do now

I'm glad you found someone

Who is more observant

Who knows

It's all about you

A life size

Fun time

One hundred forty

Some odd pounds

Of curves to cup and caress

And now, with your curiosity satisfied

Lust satiated

Throw me away

I feel less human

More latex

Every time

You tell me not to play the victim

Though you were upset when I didn't care

Are you to convince me to die for you

And refuse to take the blame?

When the day has been too long

I think back to you

Your red wasn't artificial

Nothing about you was contrived

Every night I was with the last one

I longed for you instead

Now that has ended too

And I think I'd rather be alone

Living with your ghost

Being wrapped in the shadow of your memory

Would give me greater peace

Than trying to paint over you with him

You are written across my mind

In the finest ink

I'll read our story

To pass my nights

A player like him

Lost in the cast

Because you hold all the lines

My heart remembers most

I'm trying so hard not to disappear

But it's either too much

I'm too much

Or too little

I begin to fade again

Please just tell me here and there

That you see me

Because sometimes

I can't

Annoying

Talk talk talk

Argue everything

Push away

Run away

Destroy

Burn it all down

I'm broken

I break things

And sadly

A thing is all I am

Make me pretty in your eyes

Never go digging in my backyard

You'll make a mess of everything

Hear my voice like a robin

Singing sweetly of you

Never a sharp tone

Feel I am soft to your touch

Warm in your hands and welcoming

Never a tense muscle in your embrace

Won't you love me for what you have in front of you

And not go searching any further than the surface

We'll drown if we delve that deep

It's been awhile now

That I've known

People think very little of me

If at all

I never cease to wonder why

The hurt does not desist

Inside of this mass of flesh

There is consciousness

I am real

Feeling

I exist

I am not doll parts

What did it feel like

To try me on?

You felt like smooth cool skin

Stretched over stone

You felt like pain and love

My long delicate fingers

Were small against the waves of muscle

Building up your back

My cheek to your shoulder

Or lips against your chest

As if pressed to a living statue

A little cold

Large and defined

Trying you on was like borrowing for a time

What I could never afford

You found yourself a candle

Burning bright

What a tragedy

Someone snuffed it out

With one touch

And I wished for it to come

Are we really playing this game again?

And what is my prize this time

If I should win?

A broken toy soldier

Missing a limb

No heart within

Love is a gift

And like the list of longings

You have on your mind

You may never receive it

In a panic

Racing from a nightmare

I thought I was free

My feet found quicksand

I sank slowly at first

Faster as I tried to fight it

I overcame its grip

Dusted off the debris

I looked around and saw then

Many more traps

Scattered around me

All baited with love

And so I am through with it; love

I'll step defiantly around it

Recoil from its touch

Avert my eyes from its smoldering gaze

My heart is not bitter toward love or lovers

Only indifferent

Black on black

Void of feeling

Where do the lies cease

How will this game end

Mixed with your white

Everything becomes

Grey

The only

It's not you

That's true

It's not you; you're not the one I want to love

Acutely aware

Of the countless continua

Of self

Set up staggered and jagged

Against each other

Cascades of possibilities

One, only breaths of a difference

Between the next

If I could breathe

How tragic

They turn you over in their hands

Remarking on every prism

Every bit of light reflected

And then

In a box

Lined with velvet words spoken

Promises in your ears

You will tarnish

Placed by them

Just out of reach

Where they prefer you to stay

You shone for a time

Brilliantly

After each break

I pick up the pieces

And mend them with gold

I am more beautiful all the time

Give me a little pill

Make me quiet

Still

I'll be less me

Faded, muted, a veneer

Something like a flower

Dried, pressed between the pages of a book

Beautiful to many

But to me

Only a shadow of the beauty I had in bloom

Even now

If you steep me

Long enough

I come to life

I told you

I can spin a web

With such fine threads

You gave me spools full

Every strand soaked in

Ink

Do you remember, you sang to me

About the taste of it?

You do

You bought me coffee

We went hiking

We were really friends

I thought

But I've become so tangled

In all this web

I'm spinning

Yesterday

Someone told me they saw you

That was all

They mentioned for a moment in their story

That you had driven passed them

And they went on with other topics

But I stayed there

Watching your face

As you went by

Slowly, like in a dream

This is a dream

A day dream

I've lost track of the conversation

Sometimes

I wish I was ordinary

People find beauty

In everyday mundane

Comfort in familiarity

Instead

I am odd

Not in a way that makes one

Take notice

You're like a disease

Wasn't that our joke?

I'm still sick over you

Without you here

It seems that none of the light

In this world

Is natural

Blinking, glowing, twinkling

Electric light

I miss the moon with you

Couldn't we sit up all night

Forever in hours

With just that little bit of starlight?

You liked my stories

I think you're most interesting

An enigma

A light

I don't remember exactly

When things went black

But when I came tumbling down

I crashed into you

You were tumbling too

And we had both

Been bruised

But I gave all the blame to you

Often too

If only we had fallen

Into each other

At our best

Not simply

Heart, mind, soul

Me

You wreak havoc on my being

You've left

And now it feels as though

I've already seen the ending

To this story

I still have to live it out

Some sick matrix

And you were the little pill

I'll go cypher

Getting to know you

Moth meet flame

What a meme

And losing you

Dagger to my heart

The worst pain

My heart is always racing

Not figuratively

Actually

Factually

Beating, beating, beating

And the rhythm seems familiar

Like something I should know

I should know, but I can't recall

Dum, da dum, da, dum, da dum

La foule

Oh this marvelous madness

Trapped in a waltz

Dizzying

Whimsy

Turning, turning, turning

But I should get back to what I'm doing

I was doing something, but I don't remember

Dissociate

No surrender

I want to be clever

And cunning

To see ahead

Further than the rest

I wish to know everyone's character

And intentions

To never have the wool over my eyes

Ever again

I'd love my words to all be gold

And riches

To my mark's ears

Valuable and sought after

I need these lips to be spelled

And sealed

To only speak

When my words have been properly calculated

I think I'd like to write

Just one more thing about you

I love you more now than when I loved you

You have not faded

I cannot be cured of you

I am (<u>your name here</u>)

For life